ADAPTATION

by Irene Barker

Published in the United States of America by Cherry Lake Publishing Group
Ann Arbor, Michigan
www.cherrylakepublishing.com

Reading Adviser: Beth Walker Gambro, MS, Ed., Reading Consultant, Yorkville, IL

Photo Credits:
© Nicoleta Ionescu/Shutterstock, (cartoon girl on cover and throughout book), © Shutterstock, (chameleon) cover; © Cassette Bleue/Shutterstock, speech bubbles throughout; © Eric Isselee/Shutterstock (chameleon tail), page 4, © fotandy/Shutterstock (top circle photo), © gkkhjn/Shutterstock (bottom circle photo), © Kurit afshen/Shutterstock page 5; © Kurit afshen/Shutterstock, large photo, pages 6-7; © Jana VodickovaShutterstock, inset photo, page 6; © Delpixel/Shutterstock, (giraffes), © Olga Green/Shutterstock, (giraffe pattern), page 8, © seasoning_17/Shutterstock, (turtle), © Thomas Torget/Shutterstock, (snake), © ©/Shutterstock, (giraffe), page 9; © icosha/Shutterstock, (spider photo), © BlueRingMedia/Shutterstock, (spider illustration), page 11; © Alyson W. Kast/Shutterstock, page 12, © enciktat/Shutterstock, (tiger), © Kuttelvaserova Stuchelova/Shutterstock, (flytap), © Voronchihina Mariya/Shutterstock, (plant background), page 13; © Lauren Suryanata/Shutterstock, (mossy frog), page 14; © D. Longenbaugh/Shutterstock, (top), © ZHONG HUA/Shutterstock, (bottom), page 15; © posztos/Shutterstock, (zebras), pages 16-17, © Sourabh Bharti/Shutterstock, (tiger), page 17; © frank60/Shutterstock, (top), © Frauhellen.jpg/, (caterpillar background), page 18, © Katarzyna Maksymiuk/Shutterstock, (peacock), © Eleanor Scriven/Shutterstock, (penguins), © Gert Spierenburg/Shutterstock, (water birds), page 19; © Giedriius/Shutterstock, pages 20-21

Produced by bluedooreducation.com for Cherry Lake Publishing

Copyright © 2026 by Cherry Lake Publishing Group

All rights reserved. No part of this book may be reproduced or utilized in any form or by any means without written permission from the publisher.

Library of Congress Cataloging-in-Publication Data has been filed and is available at catalog.loc.gov.

Printed in the United States of America

Note from Publisher: Websites change regularly, and their future contents are outside of our control. Supervise children when conducting any recommended online searches for extended learning opportunities.

TABLE OF CONTENTS

An Amazing Animal 4

Adaptations 8

Animals Must Eat 10

Animals Must Hide 14

Animals Need a Mate 19

Think About It 22
Glossary 23
Find Out More 24
Index 24
About the Author 24

AN AMAZING ANIMAL

Look at the cover of this book.
What animal do you see?

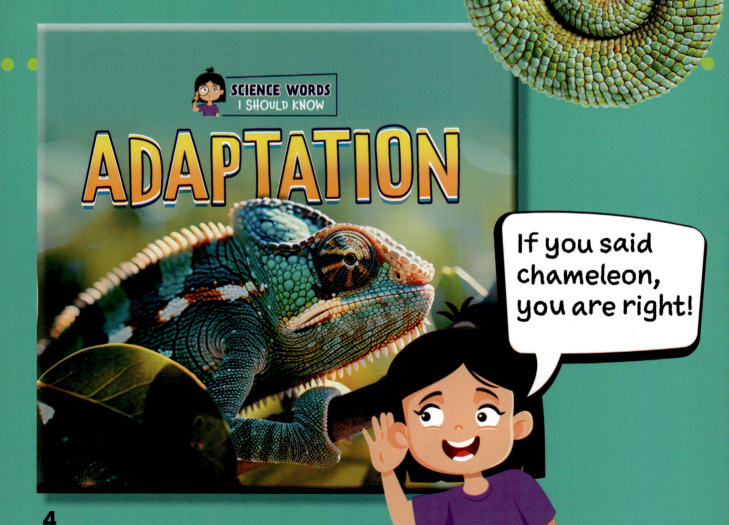

If you said chameleon, you are right!

Chameleons are amazing animals. Their skin can change colors!

Chameleons use bright colors to **attract** mates. Bright colors also warn off enemies.

chameleon: kuh-MEE-lee-uhn

Chameleons have googly eyes. They can look in two directions at once!

Chameleons are superfast at whipping out their long, sticky tongues. They almost always catch their **prey**.

1 Skin that can change colors.

2 Eyes that can see in two directions at once.

3 Long, sticky tongue to catch prey.

These are a few of a chameleon's **adaptations**.

ADAPTATIONS

Adaptations are changes that happen to animals over a long time. Adaptations help animals stay alive.

Giraffes With Short Necks?

Yes! Long, long ago, giraffes had short necks. Over time, their necks grew long. Their long necks let them eat the high leaves other animals cannot reach.

An adaptation can be a body part or a **behavior**.

A tortoise has a shell to protect its body.

A rattlesnake shakes its tail to scare enemies.

ANIMALS MUST EAT

Adaptations help animals find food. Predators hunt and eat other animals. Let's look at some of their adaptations.

A great white shark can grow to 20 feet (6 meters) long. Its size makes it one of the top predators in the ocean.

1 Powerful sense of hearing and smell to find prey.

2 Torpedo-shaped body and stiff fins for fast swimming.

3 300 sharp teeth to grab and kill prey. CRUNCH!

These are a few of a shark's adaptations.

Teeth are adaptations for eating. Meat-eating animals have sharp, pointed teeth. Plant-eaters have strong, flat teeth.

Herbivores eat only plants. Their strong, flat teeth grind food.

Meat-eaters have sharp, pointed teeth to tear their food.

Venus flytrap

A Plant That Eats Meat?

Plants have adaptations, too! Most plants have parts that use the Sun to make food. Some also have parts to trap and eat insects. The insects give them extra **nutrients**.

ANIMALS MUST HIDE

Adaptations help animals hide. Patterns on skin, feathers, or fur help animals blend in with their surroundings. We call this **camouflage**.

Can you spot the Vietnamese mossy frog? It is a master of camouflage!

1 Green and black bumpy skin to hide in mossy places.

2 Sticky toes to cling to trees and rocks.

These are two of a mossy frog's adaptations.

Gray and brown feather patterns blend in with tree bark.

Can you see the bird on the tree branch? It is a potoo.

potoo: POH-too

1 Large eyes to see at night when it hunts.

2 Stays still as a statue to hide in the day.

These are two of a potoo's adaptations.

15

Fur patterns, such as stripes, help animals hide from predators AND prey.

Zebras travel in groups called herds. In a herd, their stripes make it hard for a predator to pick out one zebra.

It is hard to see a tiger in tall grasses. Its stripes blend in with its surroundings. This helps the tiger sneak up on its prey.

Some animals pretend to be something else. We call this **mimicry**.

Is it a stick or a stick insect? It is hard to tell! Stick insects spend most of their time eating leaves and hiding from predators.

A Caterpillar That Looks Like Poop?

Yep! Giant swallowtail caterpillars look like a bird dropping. This great disguise helps keep them safe because, let's face it, no one wants to eat that.

ANIMALS NEED A MATE

Adaptations help animals find a mate. Colorful feathers, crazy dances, and gift offerings are all adaptations. Some male birds use these to attract a mate.

Peacocks fan out their long feathers to attract peahens.

A pair of water birds perform a weed dance together.

A male penguin offers a pebble to a female.

19

Most animals need a mate to **reproduce**. If the male animal has no clever tricks or gifts to offer, it may try to look the strongest instead.

A strong mate means strong babies. A strong mate can keep its partner or group safe.

Male deer use their antlers to fight to be head of the herd.

THINK ABOUT IT

Using what you have learned in this book, match each sentence to the correct picture.

1 I eat meat.

2 I use mimicry to trick predators.

3 I see well in the dark.

4 I want to attract a mate.

A.

B.

C.

D.

Answers: 1D 2B 3A 4C

GLOSSARY

adaptations (ad-ap-TAY-shunz) changes in body parts or behaviors that happen over time for survival

attract (uh-TRAKT) to capture the attention of

behavior (bih-HAYV-yur) the way someone or something acts

camouflage (KAM-uh-flahj) colors or patterns that blend with surroundings to help animals stay hidden

mimicry (MIM-ik-ree) the act of pretending to be something else

nutrients (NOO-tree-uhnts) substances that living things need to stay healthy and grow

prey (PRAY) animals that are eaten by other animals

reproduce (ree-pruh-DOOS) to produce offspring or more of something

Find Out More

Books
Dickmann, Nancy. *Masters of Camouflage*, Tuscon, AZ: Brown Bear Books, 2021

Spilsbury, Louise and Richard. *Animal Adaptations*, Minnetonka, MN: Bellwether Media, 2017

Websites
Search these online sources with an adult:

Adaptations | Animal Fact Guide

Adaptations | National Geographic Kids

Index

behavior 9, 11
body 9
camouflage 14
feather(s) 14, 15, 19
fur 14, 16
mimicry 18
patterns 14, 16
plants 13
predators 10, 16
prey 7, 10, 16
skin 5, 7, 14
teeth 10, 12

About the Author

Irene Barker has been lucky to have lived and had adventures on two continents. Her favorite memories include riding horses through rugged countryside and scuba diving in tropical ocean waters. She loves to learn and write about animals and science.